HOW TO BECOME THE CONQUEROR

HOW TO BECOME THE CONQUEROR

AMSARA SEKHITA MAI
HOLLY

Contents

This book is dedicated to people of color across the diaspora.

PREFACE

What plagues us is not our journey with our conqueror... but instead who we decide to be, what imprinted impacts we let define us, what new characteristics and values we choose to carry - after we are set free.

Mental bondage is the precipice of our state. It is the second step in the liberation of the Black man and woman in the diaspora after being released from physical shackles more than 100 years ago. However, it is vital that our position be carefully examined regarding our next steps. It is important that we review our previous movements and actions, for they have gotten us this far. Simultaneously, it is with an urgency that we examine the structures, institutions, and educational systems curated by Western civilization that we and our ancestors have lived and survived through - whose ultimate goal of its creation was to keep us "in place," and benefit from our oppression. In addition, it is imperative that we remove all romanticized materials, beliefs, ideologies, and societal and cultural structures that could be blinding us from the reality of our state in the United States and ultimately the world. This same understanding rings true for Black people all over the diaspora.

It is with a humble heart that I do my best to deliver our journey and the journey of others. That I recognize our growth, elevation, resilience, trauma, and survival tactics. Since we are a layered people, a complex and divine people- I cannot attempt to sum up our experiences in a couple of pages or in the summary of a book - and refuse to. But what I will do, is lay the first brick in my portion of the foundation. I will aid in our healing and poke holes for critical thought and evaluation. I will tell our story to the best of my ability, through the simplicity of relationships. I understand that we take our information in doses for proper digestion and that it needs to be that way in order for us to unify. I understand that our spiritual elevation and successful liberation is one that will take generations, and it will not be all at once. I also understand that generations of foundation have been laid before me, which I now stand on at this point.

How To Become The Conqueror is a deep dive into our actions as a society. It is a playbook of the behaviors we have subconsciously adopted as our own. The characteristics, and personality traits of the very people who enslaved our ancestors and whose descendants continue to uphold the institutions they created. *How to Become The Conqueror* is a beautifully descriptive and gut-wrenching display of how not to be.

1

THE AFRICAN AMERICAN

Sodomize the king!
You rip me from my crown as my knees gravel into my
own soil
I now pay homage to you
Your flesh
Your toes
Your lips
Your hands
Your eyes
Your halo

You plagued yourself!

Scope my lands and make me your Cleopatra. Pull back

my legs as you mix breed, while pressed against my own wall. Kiss my trees and swallow the same rivers you just tread. Owning my weapons and my ovaries, digging into my treasures, and dropping my gold.

Sodomize the Queen!

Separating my dignity and my body, convincing me that they don't coincide, deliberately chastising my people's disposition. Chasing the dandelions of my culture and painting demons. My mind urges resist, but my hands can't rip from your arms. Raging in a battle between fear and routine. I go rogue and crawl in return.

Sodomize the king!
In front of his Queen!
Take away that king!
Show her she's no queen!

You have no power
"I've spilled oil into your oceans and have bombed your babies," he said.
"I have separated your families and starved your parents," he said.
"I have cut down your forests and got rid of your identity," he said.
"You have nothing else but me," he said.
"I am your conqueror," he said.
"Come here," he said.

So, I did...

As he straightens his back, I slump.
As he speaks, I find needle and thread to sew my lips.
As he dreams, I recreate his images in my head.
As he discovers, I don't bother inquiring directions.

You've taken my foundation, let me please you.
Stripped from my power once forced,
now I can't lose you.
The tables have turned honey, I'm a devoted lover.
I've tried, but I can't shake it.
No need to grab, I reluctantly follow.
Can't you see??

The work I've labored, why don't you love me?
The monuments I've built, why don't you feed me
like before?
I've accepted.
My heart pulls strings and puts lies to rest.
I'm defending you.
Why don't you hold me like before?

Your cradle nursed my new wounds and I've
adjusted to your ointment.
I asked him, "Why do we go back to the people
who hurt us the most?"
He said because we as people,
Lovers,

Devotees,
Symbols,
Icons,
Flesh,
Bones,
As pillars of hope
Are sick.
I keep going back.
Coughing, soothing my illness with your
prescriptions and vaccines
Placing napkins over my nose to remedy the
red lines that direct me to my medicine
You've spilled into and rubbed on me long enough.

Accept me. I am sick with you.
So much that I lay in the hymns of your God.
So much that you can trample,
and I still manage to stand.
So much that you can't even hurt me anymore.
I am now the only detriment to myself.

You can no longer pillage the pillaged.
Look in the mirror and see that you've created
a dependent so embellished in white
you'd think my nation's surrendered.
Conqueror, I now consume you because I am you.

He told me love is not pretty and I listened.
He said it was brutal,

Me when I'm torn, hands bruised and callused.
Finishing what you started.
You are there no matter what.
By my side.
Standing through it.
Watching my moves.
As I battle the waves.
Enjoying the sweet juices of my labor.

You can say I've fallen for the conqueror.
I see the child in those scared adventurous eyes.

He took pure love from my land,
and I turned it into endurance.
Genghis Khan ain't got shit on me.

He tried to Sodomize the Queen.

2

THE CONQUEROR'S WIFE

It must be horrid to be the conqueror's wife.
To know you've devoted your life to a man of
low conduct and murderous whims.
It must be hard to breathe calmly and defend.
To know your love spills blood out of greed,
instead of sacrifice.

To bear and bleed bastard babies whom he will
never claim, and you will forever turn a cold eye
To bear and bleed new land at the price of cut-throats
and divided families
To bear and bleed what you cannot control
and now conform to

It must be challenging to be the conqueror's wife.
To sit on the sidelines as your best ideas are
passed off as his own.
To nurture chaos and act like you didn't.
You must be seething in pots of guilt disguised
and thrown under a passionless smile when a
passerby, just grin and bear it.

It must be embarrassing to root
for someone who carefully
and meticulously plots your downfall.
Who puts price tags on your organs
and counts your children?
Who successfully adorns you with
trinkets of appreciation
but keeps you powerless.
Stuck between - woman and companion, ally and enemy,
supporter and hostage.

It must be frustrating to be the conqueror's wife.
To see his attraction for your opposite
and not utter a word.
To carefully contort your features as good enough copies
- you could never be the original.
Just enough hip here and curl there to spark a reminder
of his favorite attributes of another - on you.
Exhausted by the constant change,
Running in circles to prove your worth as you
dust off his pedestal.

It must be easy to be the conqueror's wife.
To know your many plans worked.
To hide behind the curtain
while another takes the blame.
A small price for the bigger role you played.
To scream victim and cry and so many come to your aid.
Until the many realized they'd been tricked and swayed.

It must be confusing to be the conqueror's wife.
To benefit from the slaughter and have no respect.
To be forced to see your man's as bad as it gets.
For the society made in your honor to turn on you
and see you're a farce.
And the comfort shown your way is by force and scarce.

In the beginning, did she know what it would cost her?
The puppeteer, neatly laid directions embossed "sir."

But most of all, it must be sickening to realize
you've created a monster.

3

THE OTHER WOMEN

Can you tell who my conqueror is?
I've created honey in flowerpots of pollen,
I lit up the sky in his name
I've committed sin and defended treason

Asking nothing in return
I'm not even sure if he was worth it
He sure didn't say that he was

But I saw this spark of light beaming from behind
his pupil that said, "I'm here."
I stayed knowing he didn't know how to
handle his magic.
Knowing he was afraid of it.

Maybe if I cultivate it,

After all, I till my own land
And I've broken my own heart,
The second time's the charm, blame yourself
- Fool me twice.
The ocean never leaves the shore.
If your pulled to stay, you stay.

Maybe Willie Wonka was gonna congratulate me with
his Chocolate Factory for taking the entire tour.

Good women listen attentively and love hard.
Reciprocation is never relative.
I forgot about that.

Somewhere between heartache and disillusionment
- I stayed and I cried.
Like African Americans waiting on their
stamp of approval
from a plot of soil that snatched their babies
from their hands.

I will never be the conqueror's wife.

I wrapped myself in his tornado, pretending as if his arms
swept me off my feet.
I bore symphonies in his name.
Until the symphony's dried out.

I'm now scraping to find flowerpots of pollen.

Unable to remember how to extract the honey.
The sky is still lit in his name.
I've committed too many sins.
I've betrayed too many family members.
I've slept in the sheets and kissed the
forehead of the forbidden.
I've sexed out too many of his souls,
I've extracted, cleansed, and crucified the evil in him only
to find a child unable to comprehend how he got here.
Unable to take steps back.
Unable to learn from mistakes.

It doesn't matter if he was worth it.
It became clear he needed me like he needed milk.
As if my breast was the solution to help him grow.

The spark still gleamed from his eye
This time my hands couldn't cultivate the
crops I grew for his nourishment.
He stood there looking at me for food.
Empty without me.
The Conqueror. Homeless.

Revenge rested in my heart in a way France loathes Haiti.
He wanted me around but still refused
to acknowledge me for my gifts.

He was a taker

I told him I didn't want to stay - so he said, "Okay"
and then swindled his way into my arms like a gentle kiss.
A familiar hymn.
Never hearing "no"
Feeding me with the cocoa picked by the
hands of immigrant babies.
Decadence isn't sweet.
Neither is a man willing to lie, to keep.

Good women don't lie and listen in doses.

I remembered there were good moments.
Moments where I wouldn't trade you for the world.
Some I experienced on my own,
but fantasies can be real too.

I was too numb to cry.
I now expect you to fall, and grab me,
to help yourself up, then tell me you're strong.
I will not walk around silent.
I wonder what it is exactly your wife knows.
To not want me, but ejaculate freely, hold me tightly
Populate urgently, no care of pregnancy - you trust me.
Trust me to believe and share that slaves built pyramids
despite your lack of hieroglyphic proof.
Trusting that your holy religion is squeaky clean.

I don't need to be the conqueror's wife.
I know everything about you.

You wrapped yourself in my arms
knowing you'd fall asleep.
No care for my possible bastard child,
You whispered in my ear knowing I'd listen
Until my deaf ears couldn't listen anymore.
Knowing you are weak.

The Mayan Apocalypse,
How would it be if I were your conqueror?
If I used, you as my fallback?
Would you burn my flag?
Would you wave white in solidarity?
Would you fight back against my coup?
Would you accept my blankets?
Would you?

Would you innately love me?
Knowing we'd never be?

Could you love the conqueror,
Despite the wife?

4

THE CONQUEROR

You are a delusive lover
A hound thirsting for its next victim
Clear of its actions, blinded by its mission,
Plagued by its inherited bloodthirsty motives
You cannot follow anything but your patterns

Lie, Deceive, Manipulate, Divide, Weaken, and Conquer

You find strength in your structure, never seeing
it is the very thing that will topple you.
Crush you like the ego that stays when you leave.
Crumble, like castles under siege
Civilization's last breath to breathe

The walk is slow, and the voice is low and willing
A charm for charm's sake as your left hand

starts to feeling
Feeling your way through my customs and needs
Enamored by my strength and colorful beads

You take to take
Jealousy festers as you see me well
Springboarding from transatlantic tears
and wishing wells

The stare is magnetic
Sure, what you want out of your prey
Fixated on the swing of my limbs and taste of my skin
You prep yourself, to set sail on another day.

Basic in nature, ignorant in soul
Unable to grasp my depths, so you study me so

Darkness searching for the light.
Attaching yourself to the sparks that fly in the night
Desperate and greedy holding on to it for dear life
Never seeing its abundance
A child scared in fright.

You won't last long now, for we now know your ways
Never could we be you, not even on our darkest days
The reversal is upon you
A sick joke that you inbred
Has led to your demise
Making it them, over you instead

You have been hoodwinked.
Your wife is out for blood.
Your bastard's babies are multiplying
Faster than your specimen could

Land now toxic, polluted water flow
Rovers on new planets so you can safely go
Survival of the fittest
The metaverse's baby monster

Lie, Deceive, Manipulate, Divide, Weaken, and Conquer

A tortured singer, a faint splinter
A sour song, a rock and roll hipster
A gentrified hood
An institutionalization built for your good

But no one is safe.

Are you holding your breath for it to be over?

The soldier defeated, the weapon mistreated
We're no longer asking for closure.

Lie, Deceive, Manipulate, Divide, Weaken, and Conquer

How does it feel to finally see,
that you are indeed a monster.

THE SPIRIT

Joyfully I run to you
Sprinting like the speed of light
It's taken some years, but you've awakened

I keep you alive.

I am everywhere.
The heartbeat and drum that siren the call.
I am your voice
The tremble and shake on the larynx
I am your feet.
The patter that runs through the woods

Joyfully I run to you.
Come into my arms.
Let me reintroduce myself

I am the Mother of Mothers
The Father of Fathers
The Being of Beings

The electricity in your veins
Universe in your cells
Pep in your step
Fruit in your organs
Whisper in your eardrum
Answer in your dreams
Fate in your circumstance
The mercy on your soul.

I am the ground you walk on.
How the room vibrates and duplicates
Determines space and matter,
The playground for the heavens
The prayers made manifest
I am your harvest,
Growing through divine intelligence.

I am the moon pulling the tide.
The mother who takes out her breast to feed
The trance that rocks you slowly and bewitches
Gaping a passageway to your origins
Reconnecting you to your roots...
Labors selflessly
Birthing, nurturing, and rearing the child

I am devoted to the highest of high

I am your mind picking apart your thoughts.
Categorizing myths and philosophies
Deciphering truths and beliefs
Logic and knowing's
I am the words that spill from your lips
The open doors
The religion you defend, the crossroads you split
I am man's best friend.

I am your first kiss
The passion in your eyes
The laugh that heals and purges
I am your urges.
The happiness that spreads like wildfire
I imagine your deepest desires
Creating visions, before it's done
Cheering on your art and innocent fun

I am your will.
Your stable mind and clear pursuit
Your freedom and unshakable determination
The bird's eye view.
The wings expanded and brave - I am stillness.
Stretching across the body
calming your nerves

I am your protection.

I neither punish nor reward,
The karma to the switchblade
The sword that takes the wild
I humble you.
I sit on your shoulders and fight your wars
I sit in your desert and pine forest floors

I am your heart
The web of interconnected consciousness
I am the balanced scale that weighs the feather
The universal law that holds you together
I am giving you a reason to share.
To bend in humility
To love, to care

I am space and time.
Your rebirth and death
The cold potion and scattered herbs
Your cycles and lessons
I am the incarnation's reminder that they
are dealt, with caution.
I deal the cards, your life in rapid velocity.

I am your kola nuts and cowrie shells
The clanking of the coins
The Tarot to the Metu Neter
My word, transcribed
I am divine Wisdom
The answer before you ask the question

The intuition that guides your destiny

I am so many, but just one.
The omnipresence
The sacrificial lamb,
Your submission to your highest self
Your divine nature, made in the likeness and image
The Creator of the Prophets,
You call me many names
Humbly in prayer
Your Christ, your Buddah, your Yahweh, your Allah,
your Neter, your Olodumare, your Brahma, your Shiva,
your Waheguru, your Onyame and Obosom, your Lord
The unconquerable peace.

Joyfully I run to you.

I am the electricity in your veins
Universe in your cells
Pep in your step
Fruit in your organs
Whisper in your ear
Answer in your dreams
Gold in your hands
Fate in your circumstance
Mercy on your soul

I am the ground you walk on.
I am the moon pulling the tide.

I am your mind picking apart your thoughts
I am your first kiss
I am your will.
I am your protection.
I am your heart
I am space and time.
I am your kola nuts and cowrie shells
I am so many, but just one.

I am your spirit.

6

THE REVOLUTION

Wade in the water with me.

I have not died.
I have shapeshifted.
Lingering in the distance
I resurrect from the invisible force of resilience.

Whispering over your head as you plot grand plans
I rest in my people.
I have swum in their gospel waters and hip-rocked
into their rhythm and blues

I have always been here.
Dressing my angels in the names of your saints,
tucking my cowrie shells beneath my bosom.
Weaving railroads through your hair

Planning your uprisings
Giving you air to breathe.

I never die,
I told you,
I come in seasons
When you are ready
When your babies are ready to listen
When the elders are ready to pass the torch
When the ancestors nudge, "It's time."

"Give me my axe for battle," he said.
"Why an axe?" she said.
"So I can fight the lies," he said.

"So that I can resurrect as the original man.
The crème of the crop. The first. The father.
The lover. So that I can cleanse the stigma
and show God on earth. The protector and provider,
the leader and the path forger. Be the example of
divine masculinity wrapped in cocoa skin and full lips.
The balance we need."

She replied, "You don't think they already know that?"
"That is why they work so hard."

"But no, you don't understand. I have to fight," he said.

What he wanted to add, was that he noticed he was

being malnourished and pressed like high-fructose corn
syrup in the juice. The whistle that leads to noose,
policing protected popular ideals, institutions serving
"only some" under veils. The pipeline populated by
black bodies and broken sentence structure. Praise the
jump shot and 8-count number. He says his prayers and
asks for forgiveness for his sins. He don't just feel this
way, it's him and his friends. Them peace rallies don't
work, maybe things'll shake if he shows some rage.
A swift prison sentence can go down at any age.
But he needs to show his kids he can protect and engage.
A martyr if he must be, a list of memorized casualties.
The single and childless mothers just stare.
They say it's all good and expect him to go out there.
He needs his axe - the playing field's not fair.

"Fight how?" she said.
"How you think?" he said.

"Because you see. I've been walking differently," she said.

"Reprogramming my consciousness
and building my juju.
I've been talking to the dead and harvesting my light.
Extracting the wicked from my soul and
building discipline.
I understand that the first rule is power over self.
The ability to have control over my will
to shift the heavens."

"So I talk to the God in me," she said.
"I am not afraid of ritual," she said.
"I ask for guidance and live in truth," she said.
"I pray all the time. What good will that do?" he said.

"They don't know how to properly use it," she said.

What she wanted to add was that she knew if
they practiced this as a unit, they could shift
psyches and flip world structures.
Create societies that protect their daughters.
No longer dragged by the standards of pillars
not built for them. Lingering potential
tossed back like a wine glass on happy hour,
on the rocks, sugar on the rim.
Unable to heal the wounds inflicted by enemies.
Unable to Heal the wounds inflicted by themselves.
The docile agenda activated.
Clear that this is not a battle between people,
but a war in the heavens.
A great-grandmother's prayer working overtime.
A task only some can see – who patiently burden
the cross of fostering a community for a vision
they'll never experience. Taking the painstaking
steps to rewrite the future and uncover the past.
A few for the whole.
She won't lose any more babies.
Don't you get that you are magic?

"It is our secret weapon," she said.

So, I stir the pot like gumbo on Sunday.
Innately coded like the DNA that coils your hair.
Your ability to talk to music and it talk back.
The rhythm in your dance.
The beat that keeps time.
The hips when they move back and forth.

I need both of you.
For this to work, your angles need to become family.
This is a battle and a dance.
A soul and trance
Teach your children independently.
Tap into the depths of your spirits.
Stoke the fire in your abdomen.
Do the research on your own.
Manifest the affirmations.
Imagine the finished goals.
Decode the institutions.
Plant your gardens.
You are in it but not of it.
I'm so glad you are ready.
I am here now, but will be back again.

The level has elevated you only, to where you
can comprehend.

I tell you.
Your babies are ready to listen
The elders are ready to pass the torch
The ancestors said, "It is time."

With peace in your heart
A sword in your hand
Divinely you ignite The Revolution.

Words by John Henrik Clarke

"Powerful people cannot afford to educate the people that they oppress, because once you are truly educated, you will not ask for power. You will take it."

- **JOHN HENRIK CLARKE, AFRICANS AT THE CROSS-ROADS: AFRICAN WORLD REVOLUTION**

ACKNOWLEDGMENT

Thank you to the family and community that raised me. That encouraged me to be inquisitive and gave me the space to do research and make conclusions on my own. Thank you to my ancestors, whose shoulders I stand on and humbly kneel to their example. Thank you to the Neteru and Shepsu for continuing to speak to and guide me as I embark on this journey of discovery and empowerment.